Leveraging Technology

The Lessons Learned Series

Learn how the most accomplished leaders from around the globe have tackled their toughest challenges in the Harvard Business Press *Lessons Learned* series.

Concise and engaging, each volume in this series offers fourteen insightful essays by top leaders in industry, the public sector, and academia on the most pressing issues they've faced. The *Lessons Learned* series also offers all of the lessons in their original video format, free bonus videos, and other exclusive features on the 50 Lessons companion Web site: **www.50lessons.com/technology.**

Both in print and online, *Lessons Learned* contributors share surprisingly personal and insightful anecdotes and offer authoritative and practical advice drawn from their years of hard-won experience.

A crucial resource for today's busy executive, *Lessons Learned* gives you instant access to the wisdom and expertise of the world's most talented leaders.

Other books in the series:

⊰ **LESSONS LEARNED** ⊱

Leveraging Technology

LES50NS

www.50lessons.com/technology

Boston, Massachusetts

Printed in the United States of America

14 13 12 11 10   5 4 3 2 1

Library of Congress Cataloging-in-Publication Data

Leveraging technology.
     p. cm. — (Lessons learned)
   ISBN 978-1-4221-3989-9 (pbk. : alk. paper)
  1.   Technological innovations—Management.
  2.   Information technology—Management.
  3.   Industrial management—Technological innovations.
  I.   Harvard Business School. Press.
   HD45.L437 2010
   658.5'14—dc22

                                        2010004101

In partnership with 50 Lessons, a leading
provider of digital media content, Harvard
Business Press is pleased to offer *Lessons
Learned*, a book series that showcases the
trusted voices of the world's most experienced leaders. Through the power of per
sonal storytelling, each book in this series
presents the accumulated wisdom of some
of the world's best-known experts and offers
insights into how these individuals think,
approach new challenges, and use hard-won
lessons from experience to shape their leadership philosophies. Organized thematically
according to the topics at the top of man-
agers' agendas—leadership, change management, entrepreneurship, innovation, and
strategy, to name a few—each book draws
from 50 Lessons' extensive video library of
interviews with CEOs and other thought
leaders. Here, the world's leading senior

A Note from the Publisher

executives, academics, and business thinkers speak directly and candidly about their triumphs and defeats. Taken together, these powerful stories offer the advice you'll need to take on tomorrow's challenges.

As you read this book, we encourage you to visit **www.50lessons.com/technology** to view videos of these lessons as well as additional bonus material on this topic. You'll find not only new ways of looking at the world, but also the tried-and-true advice you need to illuminate the path forward.

⊸ CONTENTS ⊱

Contents

Contents

Leveraging Technology

The Impact of Technology

Sir Donald Cruickshank

Former Chairman, London Stock Exchange

NEVER FORGET THAT somewhere, in some garage or some university lab, some scientist—consciously or unconsciously—is inventing things and thinking things that will upset your business, will upset the established wisdom as to how your business runs. And that's not just true of high-tech companies. It's true of retailing companies and it's true of manufacturing companies as well. My first real experience or observation of this was almost by accident.

When I was a director general of telecommunications at Oftel, we got into a dialogue with the FCC in Washington about trans-Atlantic competition; the director of the Office of Policy and Planning at the FCC was a professor from Berkeley. He invited me to talk to some of his colleagues out there—this is early nineties—about what was happening with the Internet. It was about the digital world evolving; it was about the old world—the old analog world—disappearing. I remember in particular meeting a professor who was about to take a three- or five-year sabbatical to set up her own company, which was going to be taking her research findings on how to multiply the capacity of an optic fiber—I mean almost infinitely—by using different wavelengths of light in the practical manufacturing process. I thought, "Heavens, what does that do to the investment program that I'm trying, as director general of Oftel, to oblige British

The Impact of Technology

Telecom in the U.K. to be making in terms of its basic infrastructure?"

I began to see just how the impact of that science and this translation to practical investment projects were going to totally change the economics of not just BT, but other telecom companies.

Ever since then, at a minimum I read *Scientific American* and at a maximum take good care to search out what's happening on the frontier, as it were, of the science in the area in which I'm involved. You can see really quite large companies that are irretrievably—seemingly—locked into strategies that rely on the existing skills, the existing infrastructure, and the sunk cost of the assets. They're driven by accountants and financial metrics of the capital markets into maintaining strategies and investments that are declining in value as the work of a scientist begins to impact.

An awful lot of what's called the dot.com boom was very late realization by the major telecommunications companies that this was happening. They all simultaneously decided they had to do something about it. So, somehow, to have the information systems, management structures, and relationships with those investing in your company, to enable these intelligent investments about the new world to be made sufficiently far in advance to change the path of the company is crucial.

TAKEAWAYS

⇥ Never forget that somewhere, some-one—consciously or unconsciously—is inventing things and thinking things that will upset your business.

⇥ The value of every company's strategies and investments will diminish over time as scientific and technological advances impact business skills, infra-structures, and markets.

The Impact of Technology

⚔ It is crucial to have in place the information systems, management structures, and relationships with those investing in your company that enable intelligent investments to be made sufficiently far in advance to change the company's path.

Technology Drives New Business Strategy

Joseph Eckroth

Senior Vice President and CIO
The Hertz Corporation

PROCESS INNOVATION AND IT in the car rental industry at Hertz are inseparable. We don't talk about them separately. They're totally linked at the hip, and they are our strategy.

New Business Strategy

We have a rolling three-year strategy. We call it a strategic architecture. There are four pillars in that architecture, and technology is one of them. Process is another one, and then there are people and market strategies.

Right now, technology is more than merely the enabler of where we're going from a competitive strategy in the future. We just entered car sharing, and so we launched car sharing. The technology that we've developed in the car-sharing space is already some of the best-in-class technology, and it will differentiate the way we do business three to five years from now.

Today, car rental is typically a line item on your travel itinerary. For a business traveler, it's picking up the car wherever you're landing, using it to do your business, and then returning it. It's a line item on the itinerary. It's the same thing on your vacation.

We want to go from being just your travel itinerary line item to part of your lifestyle. In order to do that, we have to be a seamless part of your life through technology. You're enabled to interact with Hertz anytime, on your terms, from anywhere, from any device, and basically get the car of your choice where and how you need it. If that role changes from week to week or day to day, which is totally possible, it becomes more part of a community than it is just a customer-to-supplier relationship.

When you think about that from car sharing all the way through longer-term leasing, whatever you need—rent it for an hour or rent it for a year and change in between if you need to—that's only possible through technology. You can't cost competitively and you can't enable the customer to control that experience without technology. So that's our vision.

TAKEAWAYS

- In many industries today, process innovation is inseparable from the technology that makes it possible.

- In order to become a seamless part of their lifestyles, a company must enable customers to interact with it on their terms; anytime, from anywhere, and from any device.

- Successful companies recognize the flexibility of their customers' roles and needs and adapt their offerings accordingly.

- Technology is essential to enabling customers to control their own experience.

Standardize Practices Across Business Functions

Robert Herbold

Former Chief Operating Officer
Microsoft Corporation

ONE OF THE things I ran into when I joined Microsoft in 1994, after twenty-six years at Procter & Gamble, was a real organizational mess. The reason I was hired was to take the business issues off of Bill Gates's desk because he didn't enjoy doing those things. He wanted time with the products. Steve Ballmer was running sales, and I had the other things.

The first quarter I was there, two or three weeks after the end of the quarter, we still didn't have the numbers because the finance people were massaging all this data they were getting from all these subsidiaries and divisions. I couldn't understand it. I went over to the finance organization, and they showed me just what a zoo they had on their hands, because all the subsidiaries had become very, very independent.

For example, the German subsidiary had developed its own chart of accounts and hired a bunch of people to develop some new information systems. They realized their marketing budget was a little high, so they took parts of marketing and redefined it and put it up in cost of goods sold. They weren't being unethical; they were just being advocates for their work. But then you went to Italy and they did something different, and you went to the U.S. and they were handling it another way. At the end of the quarter, that all comes together, and you realize what a mess you have. We had to clean this up.

Also, the staffing was out of control. At that German subsidiary, they had over seventy IT people. This is supposed to be a sales subsidiary. They have seventy IT people, and they had built their own data center. People just get out of control when they're fairly successful, and the business was growing something like 30 percent to 40 percent a year at this stage. They had a lot of revenue to cover up a multitude of sins, and that's really what was occurring. It was clear.

Bill Gates came into my office about three-and-a-half weeks after the close of the quarter and said, "Well, what are the numbers?"

And I said, "You son of gun, you created this mess; you know why I don't have the numbers."

What did we do? We took—I took—one individual from finance who I knew had been there six or seven years and was highly experienced. He was in the controller area. And we took an IT person who was familiar with the existing systems and who had been with the company seven or eight years and said to these two individuals, okay, you're going to be the leaders of a team. The finance person is in charge, the IT person will work very closely with him, and you form a small team. And what we want to do is, first of all, in the next couple of weeks, we want you to define the chart of accounts that will be used throughout the company. We also want you to define the architecture of the systems that you're going to develop in order to clean up this mess.

In eleven months, they had rolled this thing out, and we literally were able to move out of the IT organization hundreds and hundreds of people. This is in a company that's growing 30 percent to 40 percent. They were able to eliminate hundreds of information systems, so that German subsidiary that had seventy IT people, we cut down to two. We eliminated their data

center and told them their job was to sell.
Their job is not to be creative in regard to
the general ledger and building fancy new
information systems. What we wanted to do
was the basics, and we wanted to be able to
close the books in forty-eight hours.

Well, we had all the data on one database
in Redmond, Washington. You could get
to it from these Web-based menus from
anywhere in the world. I could be in a hotel
in Hong Kong; I could be in an office in
Germany or in my office in Redmond.
I'd name the time period, the products,
and, boom, there's the key information
I needed. It was a thing of beauty.

After we finished this project, it then
became the showcase for presenting to customers how they should manage their company using Microsoft software. It turned
out to be an incredible sales tool, while also
solving this mess at Microsoft. And it was
a powerful experience to go through to
understand the power of simplicity and the
power of clear delegation of very specific
criteria as to what you want to happen.

Standardize Practices Across Functions

What did I learn from that experience? What I learned was, within these functional areas—like IT or HR or finance or manufacturing—if you let that fragment and let all the subsidiaries and divisions go off and do their own thing and then have a central group that attempts to pull this stuff together with some sanity, you are in for heavy weather. You need some crisp, standardized measures to know what's happening in the organization.

———

TAKEAWAYS

———

- When growth and revenue are high, it is easy for a company to lose control of operational efficiency.

- Teams need strong, experienced leaders with clear delegation of specific goals in order to be successful.

Leveraging Technology

◆ Overcoming its own internal challenges can powerfully position a company to understand and address the same issues for its customers.

◆ Simple, standardized structures and processes provide an organization with clear operational visibility.

How IT Can Trigger a Business Innovation

Donagh Herlihy

Senior Vice President and CIO, Avon

THIS IS AN INSTANCE for me of how IT triggered an innovation. It will be a business innovation, because in my mind there is no real, valuable innovation that's purely an IT innovation.

Leveraging Technology

We have about 6 million Avon representatives active at any point in time. They're
not employees of the company, but they're
independent entrepreneurs who sell our
products. They make money based on the
discounts that we apply in our sales to them.
The people they sell to tend to be friends,
families, coworkers—in other words, their
network. When I joined the company, what
struck me was the synergy between the ideas
of Web 2.0—social networking, social
media, and that migration of people to
online networking between individuals—
and the way our representatives work with
and sell to their customers.

I remember I was in Thailand. It was an
executive committee meeting, and it was my
second month in the company. I came back
and said, "Look, I've appointed myself as
a representative. I've gone into the field.
I've gone to the coal face."

We were talking broadly about technology
innovation and our strategies as a company.
I started talking to the executive committee
about this idea of the Web 2.0 synergy with

our business model. You could see a couple of people got it, because a couple of people were on Facebook, LinkedIn, or one of the platforms and understood the online network effect and the impact of friends and so forth. But you could see most of the people didn't get it, because they are a generation removed from the daily use of this technology.

I brought in somebody from outside the company to meet with the group, and we went through the landscape of everything Web 2.0, from blogs and wikis, social meeting platforms, and so forth. It was an education level setting exercise. At the end of that, when the committee was engaged, we posed the question again, do you see any kind of relationship between these individual consumers—how they're using technologies—and our business model? The lights were going on in people's minds. They could start to relate to it. Then it was a case of going through a process of saying, "That's fine. How do we make it grounded? Where is the business value credit for the representatives? Where's the business value credit for Avon? How is this something that's driven by a business strategy rather than just another cool technology that we play with and we experiment with?"

We did field research in four countries. We went through a strategy-setting process that was informed by the voice of the customer and some research. Then we came back to the executive committee with three concepts: mock-ups of what we felt we could do, with feedback from representatives regarding the value to them, should we able to deliver those platforms.

The key here was we were biting it off one step at a time: education, aligning people around a hypothesis, testing the hypothesis with the customers, and then doing very quick-and-dirty concepts in mock-ups. Again, we were testing that, and so at each stage of the process—the innovation process—we were narrowing in on a design, but we were not committing much funding or much resourcing up front.

TAKEAWAYS

- In order to have value, IT innovations must support the goals and functions of a business.

- When introducing new technology into a strategy discussion, know your audience and be prepared to teach them how the technology works and what value it offers.

- Use research, customer feedback, concept mock-ups, and field testing in a continuous cycle of development to innovate strategy without committing a lot of capital or resources up front.

It's Important That New Technologies Have a Champion

Irene Hrusovsky

President, CEO, and Chairman, EraGen

THROUGHOUT MY HEALTH care
career, I have been championing technology; that's my passion. I've been focused on

New Technologies Need a Champion

advancing new technologies into health care and even in large corporations at the entrepreneurial edge. You can be there in large corporations—they do allow some of us there, but you have to deliver—but one of the most critical ingredients, because these are always technologies and *new* technologies, is a champion.

There's usually a scientific champion who absolutely believes in that technology and has a vision about what the technology can do. And they will keep that vision—that belief in that technology—throughout all the roller-coaster rides that you will go through in your business. It is really important. They are not necessarily the people who are going to manage the organization or provide your director leadership or management to the team building it. But they are the ideas and the energy and the inspiration and the continued reinforcement of the technology.

I had that experience across all of the technologies I had an opportunity to work on within Abbott Labs. At Glaxo, although I wasn't there very long, I had a similar opportunity. There was always a person behind that particular application or that particular new drug. I came to EraGen, and I found the same thing. That was a critical ingredient for me to find, because if you don't have a champion, along the way your company is going to change. By necessity, it has to evolve. But early on, where you don't have traction yet and you really haven't advanced the technology applications to the point that you can see your way through with people who may have more ordinary vision or have the skill sets to actually commercialize these technologies in both real product development and commercialization, you really need that champion—the visioning champion, scientist, inventor-type person—behind you, cheering you on and providing energy and focus.

I recall a very special person. He was incredibly effective. At Abbott, we had been launching into a very new business area, with a new novel technology, so two big "news"—big for a large corporation, much more risky than one typically anticipates. We had a brilliant champion not only behind the technology but behind the application, and he was knowledgeable enough to realize that there were other people who were going to need to help shape how we got there. What is it really going to look like? What is it really going to take? So he stayed in that mode, as an adviser to the company, always ready to go both on a technical question or on the critical application question, and that worked extraordinarily well.

I think where it can go astray is when a person has that orientation as a meaningful adviser—an energized, inspirational ideas-person—but they don't recognize that perhaps the other skills are important to begin to shape those ideas and those technologies into real products for the marketplace. Or they do not recognize what's really required to get that vision accomplished. So the vision is to stay on track, but there's a lack of recognition or realistic expectation about what it takes to turn that vision into a reality.

I think the art of managing that passion and that vision is the challenge we all face, because we know we need it and we know we need it to push us forward, but we also need to be pragmatic about how we are able to implement that. The management of that vision, along with how we quantify the expectations, how we implement and execute against those expectations, and how we shape this as a real commercial entity is the other crucial side of it. So we have the promoters, champions, and cheerleaders on the one hand being very passionate, driving more quantitative aspects of the business, and on the other hand focusing disciplined implementation on execution.

TAKEAWAYS

⚄ One of the most critical ingredients for advancing new technologies through an organization and into the marketplace is a champion who provides vision, belief, inspiration, and continued reinforcement of the technology's capabilities.

- ⚑ It is important for leaders to identify technology champions because they provide consistent energy and focus amid the changing development cycles every product and company goes through.

- ⚑ The ideal champion not only advocates for the technology but appreciates the complementary skill sets required to turn vision into commercial reality.

- ⚑ In managing the passion and vision of new technology development, it is crucial for leaders to quantify expectations and execute within them as they shape the new commercial entity.

Building a Business-Focused Technology Team

Robert Fort

CIO, Vice President of Information Technology
Virgin Entertainment Group

YOU NEED TO understand the personality types that get into IT and why it sometimes becomes a challenge for them to interface with the business. It's because the people who are in IT like to build things. They like to discover things. That's the fun thing about technology.

I've always understood that technology—or an IT organization within a company—is there for the benefit of the company. When I was at a restaurant, for example, we weren't there to build the world's greatest IT department and write the world's greatest programs. We were there to sell chicken. In Virgin, we're there to sell CDs or, as we've expanded into a lifestyle brand, an entertainment lifestyle. It's imperative that the IT people start getting their heads around the idea that it isn't just for technology's sake, but it's for business's sake.

With the people who cultivate up through IT, there's going to be a whittle-down effect. Some are going to be good in the technical space and should be rewarded well for that area. But you have to find those gems who can start to understand the bigger context of what it is they're doing. It's usually people who can start to show you that they have an understanding not only of technology, but also of how technology is applied to business's benefit. Then you bring those people into your fold and try to help guide them along.

That's also why I think that businesspeople are becoming effective in coming into the IT organization as well. They already have that understanding. When you start off and think about the IT personality type who comes into the organization, many of those people are there to play with toys, to understand technology, to be detectives, to build mountains. They don't even understand why they're doing it sometimes. It's going to be the rare person who can have that complete understanding of the IT organization and its impact on business.

At the same time, I constantly try to create an environment within my organization where my folks know why it is that we're there. We're there to help sell CDs, in the case of Virgin, and now we've even moved to selling the lifestyle. That includes fashion, books, and electronics. You create an overall environment where they understand that. I received good feedback on that recently when I had a network engineer send me a text message and tell me that the router was down at one of our stores. That's IT speak. He carried on in that message and immediately pointed out to me what business processes were impacted and what they were doing to communicate to the users that it was happening.

As I read the text message, I was very pleased with what I saw. I just said, "Okay, there's nothing left to do."

It shows me that they've actually started to understand. With the router down, a typical IT person would say, "I'm going to get to fix the router." My organization understood that they actually had dollars and cents at stake, that they had people at stake. They were actually thinking in those terms and trying to communicate to them.

TAKEAWAYS

⚒ It is helpful for leaders to understand that the people who gravitate toward IT like to build and discover things, sometimes without even knowing why they're doing it, so interfacing with the business may be a challenge to them.

⚒ It is the IT manager's role to identify and cultivate personnel who can understand the bigger context of what they're doing and how technology is applied to business's benefit.

⚒ IT leaders must create within their organization an environment where people understand their impact on the business.

Embracing Technology Discontinuity

K. Vaman Kamath

Former CEO and Managing Director
ICICI Bank Limited

I WOULD LIKE to start by looking at the mid-nineties, as applicable to the banking space, or in broader context, the financial services space. Indeed, in those days, the mainframes ruled, and any application that we wanted in the banking space ran on a mainframe. We were in India, trying to induct technology into our banking operations, and the first thing that we saw at ICICI was the fact that we could not afford a mainframe because the scale of operations was small and the mainframes would make it prohibitive for us to induct technology.

The call we had to take at that point of time was, do you postpone introduction of technology or do you look at alternatives? The alternatives were what one would call a distributed process, using what can best be described as beefed-up CPUs. We ended up choosing not the mainframe, but these vastly cheaper sources of technology solutions. We were able to demonstrate within the next three to four years that these solutions met all our needs.

Not only that, but as we got into the years 2000 and 2001, when we had built up scale and could benchmark numbers, we could crank these numbers against established, much larger institutions that had globally proven that they were good at using technology. We could demonstrate that we were running technology at one-tenth the transaction cost that these companies were running at. The gain was entirely due to this decision that you could use nonstandard solutions. We run 30 million customers today, and we have no mainframe in the bank. In fact, the number of servers that we have decreases every year.

To put it in context, ten or twelve years back, we had less than 100,000 customers; we now have something like 30 million customers. This scale-up has been possible in this new continuous world by embracing a discontinuity. The discontinuity was that the mainframe regime as we knew it had ended, and a new regime was starting. You had to jump.

The challenge always is—and this is the lesson that I draw—that whenever there's a discontinuity, you see a vast open chasm in front of you. You need to then calculate whether it is feasible to jump, whether it is reasonable to jump, and whether jumping across will land you on the other side and give you new vistas or likely cause you to fall into that deeper chasm. Our own reckoning is that if you do your analysis right, you can make the decision, you can take that leap. Part of it is a leap of faith. Much of it is based on a solid foundation. The vistas beyond are indeed very welcoming.

TAKEAWAYS

- ⚎ When smaller companies are looking to implement technology but established solutions are cost prohibitive, investigating and adopting alternatives may yield greater benefits.

- ⚎ Whenever there's a technology discontinuity, you see a vast open chasm in front of you and you need to calculate whether it is feasible to jump, whether it is reasonable to jump, and whether

Embracing Technology Discontinuity

jumping across will land you on the other side and give you new vistas or cause you to fall into the chasm.

ᚎ If you do proper analysis, you can make the decision and take that leap; part of it is a leap of faith, much of it is based on solid foundation, but the rewards can be great.

━━◆◆◆━━

Innovate to Disrupt an Industry

━━◆◆◆━━

Ravi Kant

Managing Director, Tata Motors

NANO WAS CREATED when our chairman, Ratan N. Tata, observed that there were many people, many families, who traveled on two-wheelers. Because of lack of access to four-wheelers, most people in India prefer to use two-wheelers, and today nearly

Innovate to Disrupt an Industry

8 or 9 million two-wheelers are sold in the country.

Now, you'll find—and it's a common sight in India—you'll find the whole family traveling on a two-wheeler. That means there is a husband who's sitting on the seat, there's a child that's standing in front, and there is his wife or lady sitting at the back with a child in her lap. You'll surely understand that this is a very unsafe, uncomfortable way of traveling. Mr. Tata thought if we could have a four-wheeler that would give them safety and comfort, then it could be a good segment to get into. The only condition was that it had to be accessible in terms of economical value to a large number of people, if they wanted to shift over from a two-wheeler to a four-wheeler. That was the basic concept that Mr. Tata initiated some time ago.

At a press meeting in Geneva, one of the reporters or correspondents asked Mr. Tata about this vehicle, "What do you think the price would be?" At that point in time, two-wheelers were around 40,000 rupees, and

the cheapest four-wheeler was at 200,000
rupees, so he just said 100,000 rupees,
which in Indian terminology means one
lakh. One lakh is 100,000 rupees. That
label got stuck, that it has to be one lakh,
which is equal to U.S.$2,500. That is why,
when we unveiled it in January 2008, and
when Mr. Tata was asked what the price
would be, he said, "A promise is a promise,"
and he declared that it would be 100,000
rupees. That shocked people, because
nobody expected that a vehicle at this price
could ever be produced.

It is a vehicle that is good to look at. It has
four doors; it can comfortably seat four
people. It is nice to drive; it will give a
tremendous amount of fuel efficiency—50
miles per gallon—and be economical to
use. So it has all the ingredients, and you
can understand how for the middle class,
consisting of about 350 million or 400
million people, it's a dream come true.
They could never have thought that they
would be able to ride a four-wheeler, and
suddenly, they find that they can reach
there, and they can do it. It has brought

about a huge groundswell of interest in this vehicle.

The key lesson, first, is to dream a dream. You've got to start from there. Don't think that anything is impossible. In this case, we didn't go about trying to upgrade a two-wheeler or downgrade a passenger car. We took a plain sheet of paper and started working on that. We said, if the price is going to be this, then the total cost of the vehicle has to be this. Then we broke down those costs into various components and various aggregates—the cost has to be that—that's how we began to start working, and that's how we began to start talking to all the suppliers.

I must say, many suppliers took this challenge, many multinational companies that would never have thought that they could deliver a product, a component, at that price. They looked at the whole project as totally new, looked at the whole thing out of the box, and they came up with fantastic solutions.

It's the combination of all this that has made Nano possible at this price.

TAKEAWAYS

- ⚜ Dream a dream and don't think that anything is impossible.

- ⚜ Rather than reinventing an existing product, start working from a blank sheet of paper.

- ⚜ Real innovation has the power to create new collaborations and disrupt an industry.

The Changing IT Skills Mix

Paul Jeffreys

Director, Information Technology
Oxford University

AS SERVICES BECOME more and more
mission critical in a university, the types of
skills that the staff need to offer change.

Whereas in the past, many of the services
that were built were built bottom-up, using
the computational skills of people who en-
joyed the technical aspects, increasingly, the

skills that we need now are the ability to run the very large, purpose-built systems that you buy in, even possibly managing services that are provided on the cloud or outside university, not even run at all on the university. And then, the whole series of ITIL-type (information technology infrastructure library) quality services to provide really top-line service to the user, day in and day out, are the skills that are increasingly needed, rather than the original technical skills.

When you then deliver a central service that is professional—which is as good as you would find in companies outside academia—and these are run from the center, and the wider university sees the advantages of picking them up, then the local IT staff can specialize in the areas that the units deliver. So we're hoping that three-quarters of the IT staff who are not in the center will be able to give more and more tailored support for their local users built on top of the central services that are running.

I see a real change of skills mix to having quality of service in running large enterprise

The Changing IT Skills Mix

software suites and then support for being much closer to the type of activity that happens in local units. This change leads to some challenges in terms of the staff that we have in the university. And you have to be realistic. You have to go to the staff and say, "Look, life has changed. We are here to deliver a service to the users. We have to have the right skills, the right types of people for the services that are now needed."

There's always the opportunity to retrain, to learn new skills, to be ready. There will be some areas where the traditional technical skills are still needed. A particular aspect of that is identity management and providing the underpinning directories, so it's not as though everything has stopped. For those who are really hard-line technical people, there are still challenges. But overall, you have to look for a change in the skills.

Another thing that I did when I moved to the university was set up an improved appraisal process, where we look at the training that people have done and then plan training for the future, plan careers so that we can look to see their trajectories, where they're moving, and just face the fact that, actually, the workforce has to change. There's up to a 10 percent change of staff every year, so there's flexibility of recruiting the skills that you want rather than just changing the existing skills.

TAKEAWAYS

- ⚔ The IT skill sets needed to build a bottom-up service organization are different from the skills needed to manage large, purpose-built systems that may run within or outside of your organization's IT platforms.

- ⚔ Organizations must be realistic in identifying and staffing for the changing skill sets that new services require.

The Changing IT Skills Mix

⚔ One practical way to recognize that the IT workforce must change is to adopt an appraisal process that assesses current staff training and plans for future training and career progression.

⚔ Where it is not practical or desirable to change existing skill sets in staff, it can be useful to recruit for new skills through attrition.

User Buy-in Is Key to Successful Innovation

Bruce Winzar

CIO, Loddon Mallee Health Alliance
Executive Director of Information Services
Bendigo Health Care Group

FOR A NUMBER of years, I've been interested in video conferencing. Video conferencing from a business perspective has traditionally been based around administrative use. I thought that we should be able to utilize video conferencing within a specialist care mode, where we can change the model of care. What we looked at was how we bring video conferencing into the hospital to provide specialist care to a range of remote hospitals or regional hospitals because one of the biggest challenges faced by regional hospitals is to bring specialists into the region. They certainly will not move from metropolitan areas into the country areas.

We applied for some funding, and we received some government grant funding. We moved down the line of developing a high-speed broadband network from four regional remote hospitals to four metropolitan hospitals. The project was about delivering business benefit, quality patient care, and the removal of some of the costs to transfer patients within a remote location via ambulance to a metropolitan location. We had a number of business drivers that we ticked off.

What we found was that the specialists in the metropolitan hospitals were extremely motivated to assist their counterparts in country areas. What we didn't anticipate was probably some jealousy or resentment that the specialists would want to work and help within a regional context. While we had a range of supportive CEOs, supportive senior clinicians, and in some instances young general practitioners (GPs) or visiting medical officers who were straight out of the university, all understanding the technology, we just couldn't bring the older generation of GPs to the table. That is still the case. It's an issue with country areas and regional areas where the older GPs certainly aren't technology-savvy and aren't necessarily interested in playing with some of the new technologies.

Our virtual trauma care project is totally innovative. It's one of only two or three within Australia. But if we don't look at the changed management processes, if we don't allocate enough time to the workflow, and we don't allocate enough time in bringing the user along with us, then the project, while it's quite technologically advanced, will fail.

TAKEAWAYS

- ⚔ It is important to consider the perspective of all constituents when introducing new technologies into a business.

- ⚔ People who are not technology-savvy may have a harder time adapting to the introduction of new technologies into established procedures.

- ⚔ Advanced technology initiatives can fail if a company doesn't plan change management processes and if it doesn't allocate enough time to including the user and to understanding workflow.

———◆———

Changing a Culture to Create a New Market

———◆———

John Abele

Cofounder, Boston Scientific

THIS LESSON IS something that I didn't
realize was a lesson until quite a while after
it happened.

Changing a Culture

We had developed a product called a steerable catheter. One of the applications developed in the early 1970s for the product was a technique for the nonoperative removal of gallstones. Another doctor in the U.K. had developed a different technique: he'd used an endoscope to do the same thing. Ours was guided by X-ray; his was guided optically, by fiber optics in the tube.

We decided that it would be interesting to see how these two techniques compared, so the doctors came up with the idea: "Why don't we have a competition?" This was in 1975, and we had this competition at the Middlesex Hospital in London. The contest was called a draw because the endoscopic technique was elegant, fascinating, a tour de force to see, which the audience appreciated. But the radiologic technique was simple and could be applied by anyone, because the skills were very easy to learn. It was an important educational technique.

That experience, as it turns out, didn't influence the market right away, but over a number of years, others started to copy that technique and said, "Using this technique we can teach much more rapidly than we have done traditionally. Not only that, if this course that we teach is not sponsored by an establishment institution—the academic center or a professional society—then we don't have to worry about being politically correct and influencing people. We will have a course where there will be a live demonstration everybody can see, and there will be a panel of experts commenting on this case continuously."

In addition, everybody in the audience was equipped with a keypad. And sometimes these audiences would range up to ten thousand physicians, so it was a big, big deal. You in the audience would see a procedure being done. You could see not only the patient and the physician, but also inside the body, because they would have X-rays or endoscopic pictures. You would see recent publications on the technique, clinical trials—both for and against so you'd get a balanced representation of what a lot of people think—and then you'd hear experts arguing about it. That enabled you to have a real-time peer review.

In addition to the peer review of experts, you would also have the peer review of all your colleagues, who were answering questions in parallel with the presentation. Questions are posted silently on a screen; you press a button to answer it, like you do in some television programs, and the answer comes out. You can answer anonymously. Nobody will know how you've voted, but you will know how all of your colleagues thought at the same time. Because this is continuous and you are all learning, you will see how minds are being changed.

What makes this interesting and why this became a lesson for me after the fact is the fact that, at Boston Scientific, we were constantly introducing very disruptive technology. By disruptive, I don't just mean new: disruptive means that you have to learn new skills. Sometimes you are going to have to change the players, and if you do, you'll need new infrastructure. The economics are different, and the pathways in and out of the system are different. This is very threatening to the establishment, where the normal response would be, "Let's write about them," and "Show me your twenty-year results," which is exactly what they did.

But this was an example where the physicians started voting with their feet. They said, "I want to go to this independent course because I learn more, and I think I trust this information more than the courses that are put on by my professional society."

For us, it collapsed the time frame for the development of these new technologies because they don't spring perfectly formed into the marketplace; they go into the marketplace and then they constantly evolve and iterate. This medical live demonstration course enabled us—as technologists, not just as companies—to learn more and to understand not only the technical aspects, but also the social, economic, and political aspects as well, which is essential if you're going to change a culture and create a new market.

TAKEAWAYS

- ⚐ Innovations in technology can lead to powerful innovations in teaching and in learning the skills necessary to use it.

- ⚐ The iteration of technology can benefit from being independent of established markets and of affiliations with particular organizations or agendas.

- ⚐ To change a culture and create a new market, it is essential to learn and understand the technical, social, economic, and political aspects of new product development.

Creating a Unique Multichannel Customer Experience

Howard Lester

Chairman and CEO, Williams-Sonoma

WHEN WE STARTED, I was very fortu-
nate in that we had a company whose rev-
enues were 50 percent from catalog and

A Multichannel Customer Experience

50 percent from stores. So maybe we just assumed that was the way it ought to be. We initially grew the business with the catalog those first four or five years, so when we went public in 1983, we were 80 percent direct and 20 percent in stores. We only had, I think, five or six stores when we went public: the four initial and a couple of test stores.

But over the years, we began to understand the power and the synergy of having the two channels, and we wanted to develop a strategy that would cause the customer to shop both channels with us, if possible. We observed other retailers that did the same thing—had catalogs and stores—but their catalogs were mirror images of their stores. When that happened, one of them dried up, either the catalog or the store. More often the catalog suffered. A couple come to mind.

Sharper Image was a very hot retailer here in the early eighties. There were lines to get into their stores. They were serving the well-to-do yuppie in those days. But as they opened stores, their catalog, which had been their dominant channel, drifted away to nothing because the store was a mirror image of the catalog. So, why did the customer need to shop the catalog? They would go to the store because they liked to ask questions and get their hands on the merchandise.

The same thing happened to Brooks Brothers, which used to have a wonderful catalog business. But as they started to open more stores, the customer went to the store because of size, fit, and color. And so they lost them.

Having observed that, we developed the strategy that the catalog for Williams-Sonoma would be an item business. The idea was that we would have items in there, we would have a lot of ideas in there, a lot of recipes in there. The store would be an assortment business. And we would have some items in the catalog that weren't in the stores, so that the customer would have a unique experience in each channel. And hopefully if they got the catalog, which was our advertising vehicle, that would

A Multichannel Customer Experience

also encourage them to go to the store
for more, if we began to convince them
that this was a lifestyle that they wanted to
participate in.

That has been our strategy, which I think
has worked well for us and has kept both
channels vibrant. And actually, after we
built almost six hundred stores, we still do
40 percent of our business in the direct
channel today. It's been that way probably
since the late eighties. After we started
building some stores, we went to about a
sixty-forty mix, and it's continued to be
amazing really to me that our direct business
has remained so vibrant to the point that
today, in 2005, we'll mail about 400 million catalogs. And when you consider there
are a little over 100 million households in
America, that's a lot of catalogs. But each
year we mail more catalogs than we did
the year before, plus we've diverted some
of the catalog business now to the Internet,
to the Web, which is also a very vibrant
business for us and part of that direct total
of 40 percent that I mentioned.

Leveraging Technology

All of our businesses follow the same pattern. We start it with a catalog. If it's appropriate, we open stores. But in the main, we do the catalog, we do a Web site now, and we do the stores. And we have a different strategy for each business in terms of the assortment and how it bounces off the other channels.

What we want to achieve is a synergistic strategy and a different experience on each of the channels for our brand. Now, that goes against a lot of people's conventional wisdom, which is, let's give them the same experience on every channel. But we believe it's very important to maintain that all channels continue to have a vibrant, unique experience for the customer, because your best customers will shop all the channels.

TAKEAWAYS

- ⚔ When using more than one channel to reach customers, differentiate the nature of their offerings to maximize profitable customer interaction.

- ⚔ Each channel must offer a vibrant, unique customer experience in order to thrive in its own right.

- ⚔ Use technology to expand, not replicate, your business strategy into new opportunities for growth.

Using Technology to Get Closer to Your Customers

John Clarke

Senior Vice President and CIO, Nokia

ONE OF THE areas that, for me, demonstrates where we best led IT innovation within the business was when I was working within retail as a CTO. What we recognized there with the business is that we had staff in a store, hidden away, doing their work behind the scenes in the back office. Customers were stuck in the store with questions. The opportunity there was how to bring the two together?

What we looked at was: how do we completely mobilize the staff so they can do all their work in the aisle directly in front of the customer, and, should the customers have a question—and they did—the staff would be there? Also the staff wouldn't need to—and they did in some cases—run backwards and forwards all day long to a green screen. They could do all their work far more seamlessly.

So we completely mobilized their work activity to a mobile device in a store. That had a fantastic impact on store morale and an even better impact on customer satisfaction. Customers always felt there was somebody there they could ask a question of. By doing that, there was a huge increase in productivity. One was it saved them a lot on shoe wear. Staff would spend, in some large stores, a lot of time and footwear going to and fro, trying to get answers.

It also let them do their jobs, check on the stock level, check on the range, and print off some papers, because they had belt printers as well. It let them do all that at the point where there might be a problem and then they could respond to customers in real time. It just made them far more effective. They did that by being next to the customer, and staff likes to be with customers generally.

My lesson from this was, do not underestimate the benefits of getting your workforce closer to the customer, letting them use technology to do that, but letting them do the work with the customer. It lets them understand what the customer feels, their frustration or their happiness, but also lets them deal with any needs customers may have.

TAKEAWAYS

- ≒ Aligning mobile technology with the needs of your workforce can boost morale and improve customer satisfaction.

- ≒ Mobility through technology increases both productivity and efficiency.

- ≒ Don't underestimate the benefits of bringing your workforce into the same space as your customers.

Avoid Rigid Thinking

Jimmy Wales

Founder, Wikipedia and Wikimedia Foundation

THE HISTORY OF Wikipedia says something about the great impact of rule breaking.

Before Wikipedia, I had a project called Nupedia. Nupedia had the same broad vision, the same idea that excited people, which was to create a free encyclopedia for every single person on the planet, in their own language. That broad, unifying idea got a lot of people excited, and they came in to start working on this.

The model we designed at that time was very top-down. There was a seven-stage review process in which people had to fax in their degrees so that they could prove their credentials. The process was very old fashioned, but it was also old fashioned for a reason. It wasn't old fashioned just because we wanted to be old fashioned; it was old fashioned because we thought that's how you would build an encyclopedia. This was a complete failure. We put a ton of money into it and two years of really hard work, and we had very little to show for it.

Then we discovered the wiki editing idea, which had been around for several years at that time. Wikis were an online phenomenon, low-key. A few programmers were using wikis. It was a subculture. Harnessing that idea and saying, "OK, let's take this completely radically open thing and now let's start building an encyclopedia with that," was really contrary to everything that we previously thought would work. And we didn't just randomly decide it; it grew out of my frustration in talking with the volunteers who were trying to build the encyclopedia. I would ask, "What's wrong? Why is it taking so long?"

So I said, "Let's just blow all that away and have a totally open-ended model instead of a priori figuring out what we think the right path is. Then, as we see problems arise, we'll think about how to solve them."

As it turned out, partly because our community grew out of the dot-com crash, there was no funding. Anytime a problem arose where we naturally thought we needed to have staff members to do x or y, there were no staff members. We had to evolve ways for the community to do it. That's what really led us, as an ever-growing and large group, to this model of radically open-ended, radical content generation by the general public.

One of the main lessons that I draw out of the story of the transition from Nupedia to Wikipedia is, avoid excessive a priori

Avoid Rigid Thinking

thinking. We had a lot of ideas about what this project would look like, how we would create an encyclopedia, and tried to a priori design the whole thing to match that preset idea. It turns out we were wrong about several things and right about a few things. The excessive a priori thinking led us to believe we had to proceed in a certain route, but we didn't.

The lesson that I learned from that is, whenever possible, if you don't have to make a decision today, then don't. Wait. Leave things open-ended and try to pursue a path so that you can make that decision at a future juncture when you need to. This has a broad applicability in many contexts. If you a priori imagine everything and then you pursue it in a very rigid way, you can get off track before you can realize it and never get back.

TAKEAWAYS

⚞ When undertaking technological innovation, be open to figuring some of
   it out as you go along.

⚞ You can hamper progress by sticking
   to preset and predetermined ideas
   about what you should do and how you
   should do it.

⚞ If you don't have to make a decision
   today, leave things open-ended and
   pursue a path that allows you to make
   that decision when you need to.

———◆———

Successfully Implementing New Technology

———◆———

Clayton Christensen

*Robert and Jane Cizik Professor of Business
Administration, Harvard Business School*

WHEN YOU HAVE a new technology,
almost always the successful implementation
of the new technology comes when you
compete against nonconsumption: use
the technology in an application where

previously the customer's only alternative was nothing at all. That way, the new technology can delight the customer, and all it has to do is be better than nothing.

If you try to implement a new technology in an established system, the only way it can be used there is if it's better than the old way of doing things in those applications. Typically, there is a very onerous technical hurdle to overcome there, whereas here all you have to do is make something better than nothing.

One example is when the transistor disrupted the vacuum tube. RCA, the leading consumer electronics company at the time, and the other vacuum tube product manufacturers all took licenses to the transistor from RCA. But the transistor couldn't be used in the market that existed for consumer electronics in the fifties and sixties. These were huge floor-standing televisions and tabletop radios.

So they took their licenses to the transistor into their own labs. In today's dollars, they spent well over a billion dollars trying to make the transistor good enough that it could handle the power required to make big floor-standing TVs and radios.

While they were working on that problem, Sony came into the market with a very different orientation. It made a very cheap, simple, pocket radio that sold for U.S.$2. Sony sold it to the low end of humanity, people we call teenagers today. Teenagers were delighted to have this crummy, simple, pocket radio because it was infinitely better than no radio at all, which was the alternative they'd been living with. I was raised in Salt Lake City, and I remember when I had my first Sony radio. I actually had to stand facing west, which was where the radio tower was, in order to catch the signal. It was really a crummy product.

Sony went next to little portable televisions that were so cheap and simple that people whose wallets weren't big enough to buy a big floor-standing RCA TV or whose apartments weren't large enough to have a big floor-standing TV now could have this little thing. And because it was infinitely better than nothing, customers were delighted.

Ultimately then, solid-state electronics, commercialized by Sony and people like that, got to the point that now they could start to make big TVs and radios with it. And then, suddenly, all the customers got sucked out of the vacuum tube world into the new. And every vacuum tube company got vaporized.

This happens over and over again in our studies of innovation. The leaders typically try to cram the disruptive technology into head-on competition with the old technology in the market that they serve. Really, if you want to commercialize it successfully and create new growth, you have to come out and use the technology to make simple, inexpensive products that are infinitely better than nothing.

TAKEAWAYS

- ⚔ The successful implementation of new technology almost always comes when it competes against nonconsumption, that is, when it is used in an application where previously the customer's only alternative was nothing at all.

- ⚔ If you try to implement new technology into an established system, you must overcome the challenge to be better than the old way of doing things in order to be adopted.

- ⚔ To successfully commercialize disruptive technology and create new growth, you have to begin by using it to make simple, inexpensive products that are just better than nothing.

ABOUT THE CONTRIBUTORS

John Abele is the cofounder of Boston Scientific Corporation, the worldwide developer, manufacturer, and marketer of medical devices. Mr. Abele has been driving the advancement of less-invasive medical technology for more than twenty-five years.

The history of Boston Scientific began in the late 1960s, when Mr. Abele acquired an equity interest in Medi-tech, Inc., a research and development company focused on developing alternatives to traditional surgery, where he served as President. In 1979, Mr. Abele partnered with Pete Nicholas to buy Medi-tech, and together they formed Boston Scientific Corporation. Since its public offering in 1992, Boston Scientific has undergone an aggressive acquisition strategy, assembling the lines of business that allow it to continue to be a leader in the medical industry. Mr. Abele has been a Director of Boston Scientific since 1979.

Mr. Abele serves as Director of Color Kinetics, Inc., a leader in designing and marketing innovative lighting systems based on light-emitting diode (LED) technology. He has held the chairmanship of FIRST (For Inspiration and Recognition of Science and Technology) Foundation since 2002.

Clayton Christensen is the Robert and Jane Cizik Professor of Business Administration at the Harvard Business School, with a joint appointment in the technology and operations management and general management faculty groups. His research and teaching interests center on managing innovation and creating new growth markets. He has been a faculty member since 1992.

A seasoned entrepreneur, Professor Christensen has founded three successful companies. The first, CPS Corporation, is an advanced materials manufacturing company that he founded in 1984 with several MIT professors. The second, Innosight, is a consulting and training company focused on problems of strategy, innovation, and growth that Christensen founded with several of his former students in 2000. Innosight Capital, the third firm, was launched in 2005. From 1979 to 1984, he worked with the Boston Consulting Group (BCG). In 1982, Professor Christensen was named a White House Fellow and served as assistant to U.S. Transportation Secretaries Drew Lewis and Elizabeth Dole.

Professor Christensen holds a BA with highest honors in economics from Brigham Young University (1975), and an MPhil in applied econometrics and the economics of less-developed countries from Oxford University (1977), where he studied as a Rhodes Scholar. He received an MBA with High Distinction from the Harvard Business School in 1979, graduating as a George F. Baker Scholar. He was awarded his DBA from the Harvard Business School in 1992.

Professor Christensen is the author or coauthor of five books, and his writings have won a number of awards.

John Clarke is Senior Vice President and CIO for Nokia, the Finnish company that is the world leader in mobility, driving the transformation and growth of the converging Internet and communications industries.

Mr. Clarke has more than twenty years of experience working in the IT industry. In his role as CIO at Nokia, he is responsible for Nokia's process and IT development activities. Mr. Clarke believes that customers are the most important factor in the current success and future growth of the company.

Prior to joining Nokia, Mr. Clarke was the Group Technology Director for Tesco, the U.K.'s largest and the world's fourth-largest retailer. He is a regular conference presenter, with an active interest in information and business analytics, mobility, and social networking. He is an active participant in security and privacy forums and is a Director with the U.K. ePassports body.

Mr. Clarke is a qualified engineer from the University of Kent at Canterbury and is an MBA graduate from Warwick Business School. He was named Finnish CIO of 2009 by *Tietoviikko*, a leading Finnish IT publication, and by *CIO* magazine.

About the Contributors

Sir Donald Cruickshank is the former Chairman of the London Stock Exchange and a current Director of Qualcomm (since June 2005).

Sir Donald was a consultant at McKinsey before joining Times Newspapers as Commercial Director, then moving to the role of Managing Director of the information and entertainment division of Pearson.

In 1984, he became Managing Director of the Virgin Group, where he spent the next five years.

He was Chief Executive of the National Health Service in Scotland from 1989 to 1993, then became Director General of Oftel, a position he held from 1993 to 1998. He spent three years as Chairman of Action 2000, the U.K. Government's Millennium Bug campaign.

Sir Donald was appointed by Chancellor Gordon Brown to be Chairman of the government's review of the U.K. banking sector in 1998. His report was published in March 2000.

He became Chairman of the London Stock Exchange in May 2000, a position from which he stepped down in July 2003.

Sir Donald has also served as Chairman of SMG from 1999 to 2004, Formscape Group Ltd. from 2003 to 2006, and Clinovia Group Ltd. from 2004 to 2006.

Joseph Eckroth is the Senior Vice President and CIO of The Hertz Corporation, the world's largest general-use car rental company, a position to which he was appointed in 2007. Hertz is a global

About the Contributors

operation with licensee locations in Africa, Australia, Europe, Asia, Latin America, the Middle East, and North America. Hertz has over 7,000 locations in 145 countries.

Mr. Eckroth received his MBA from Pepperdine University and a BS from the University of La Verne. He began his career by serving in a variety of technology and quality assurance positions at Northrop Grumman Corporation from 1985 until 1996. In the years following his time at NGC, Mr. Eckroth served as an IT executive for General Electric. Continuing there until 2000, he also served as CIO for GE Medical Systems and GE Industrial Systems business units.

From GE, Mr. Eckroth moved to a position as CIO at Mattel, Inc., the world's largest toy manufacturer. Five years later in 2005, he joined New Century Financial Corporation as CIO, later becoming Executive Vice President and Chief Operating Officer.

In his current position at Hertz, Mr. Eckroth is responsible for restructuring the company's IT operations to create a more user-friendly interaction as well as broader applications to business priorities. Additionally, Mr. Eckroth serves on the board of directors for VWR International, a medical and scientific supply distribution company.

Robert Fort is the CIO and Vice President of Information Technology at Virgin Entertainment Group, where he is responsible for developing the company's strategic direction, IT innovation, prioritization, and operations. He directed and implemented the shift to real-time reporting on customer traffic, sales, and inventory. Virgin is known as a leading branded, venture capital organization and is one of the world's most recognized and respected brands. Conceived in 1970 by Sir Richard Branson, the Virgin Group has grown successful businesses in sectors ranging from transportation, travel, financial services, leisure, and music to publishing and retailing.

Mr. Fort launched his career in 1993 with a management position at Nestlé USA, Inc., where he oversaw SAP and EDI applications. In 1996, he became Vice President of Information Technology and CIO at quick-dining restaurant company Koo Koo Roo. Two years later in 1998, he moved to Alesis Studio Electronics as Director of Information Services. From 2000 to 2003, Mr. Fort worked with international dietary and nutrition supplements manufacturer Resource Connection. As CIO, he was responsible for developing the company's annual strategic plans and implementation of a high-performance team culture.

A member of the National Retail Federation CIO Council, in 2005 Mr. Fort was named one of the Top 15 Pacesetters by *RIS News* magazine. In 2006, he was listed as *Computerworld*'s Premier 100 IT Leaders. Most recently, Mr. Fort was recognized again by *RIS News* magazine, this time as a 2008 Top 10 Influential Retail Executive.

About the Contributors

Robert Herbold is the former Chief Operating Officer and Executive Vice President of Microsoft Corporation and the Managing Director of the consulting business Herbold Group LLC.

Mr. Herbold joined Microsoft in 1994 as Chief Operating Officer and Executive Vice President. For the following six-and-a-half years, he was responsible for finance, manufacturing and distribution, information systems, human resources, corporate marketing, market research, and public relations. During his tenure as COO, Microsoft experienced a fourfold increase in revenue and a sevenfold increase in profits.

From spring 2001 until June 2003, Mr. Herbold worked part-time for Microsoft as Executive Vice President, assisting in the government, industry, and customer areas.

Prior to his time at Microsoft, Mr. Herbold spent twenty-years at Procter & Gamble. During his last five years with P&G, he was Senior Vice President of Advertising and Information Services, responsible for the company's worldwide advertising and brand management operations, all marketing-related services and management information systems worldwide.

Mr. Herbold serves on the board of directors of Agilent Technologies, Indachin Ltd. Hong Kong, and First Mutual Bank. He recently authored the book *Seduced by Success: How the Best Companies Survive the 9 Traps of Winning*.

About the Contributors

In 2001, Mr. Herbold was appointed by President Bush to the President's Council of Advisors on Science and Technology. He currently chairs the council's education subcommittee.

Donagh Herlihy is Senior Vice President and CIO of Avon. Avon is a leading global beauty company, with more than $10 billion in annual revenue, and the world's largest direct seller.

Mr. Herlihy leads Avon's information technology strategy and operations globally. He is responsible for providing all aspects of the technology infrastructure supporting Avon's internal business operations and for connecting and enabling the business worldwide.

Mr. Herlihy joined Avon in March 2008 from his position as CIO at Wrigley Company. In addition to leading IT, Mr. Herlihy also served successively as Vice President of Human Resources and Vice President of Supply Chain Strategy and Planning. During his seven years at Wrigley, he transformed IT from thirty geographically dispersed country-led organizations into a single global business unit, leveraging resources while being strategically aligned to key business drivers. He drove the transformation of Wrigley's organization and business processes, enabled by a global implementation of SAP. He developed and implemented an IT strategic planning process with strong governance over technology investments.

About the Contributors

Prior to Wrigley, Mr. Herlihy spent six years in various positions at Gillette, which was acquired by Procter & Gamble in 2005. Earlier in his career, Mr. Herlihy was based in the U.K., where he worked in manufacturing, business process reengineering, and information technology in both the consumer goods and automotive sectors.

A native of Ireland, Mr. Herlihy has both a BSC and an MA in industrial engineering from Trinity College in Dublin, and he has completed the Executive Program at the University of Michigan, Ross School of Business.

Irene Hrusovsky is the President, CEO, and Chairman of the Board of EraGen Biosciences, a molecular diagnostics company.

Dr. Hrusovsky joined EraGen in 2002 with more than twenty-five years of experience in general biomedical business management. Prior to joining EraGen, she held executive positions at both Abbott Laboratories, where she spent more than twenty years, and Glaxo. While at Glaxo, she helped to develop new business models for its merger with Smith Kline.

She received her Doctor of Medicine degree from the University of British Columbia in Vancouver, as well as BS degrees in biochemistry and genetics.

In 2006 Dr. Hursovsky was elected to the board of eMetagen, a drug development firm.

About the Contributors

Paul Jeffreys is Director of Information Technology and Professorial Fellow at Keble College, Oxford University. He works in the new e-Research Centre, which he helped create, within the maths and physical sciences and life sciences division. Mr. Jeffreys is also Co-Director of the e-Horizons Institute within the James Martin 21st Century School.

In 1979, Mr. Jeffreys started his career as a CERN Fellow in the experimental physics division. He began working at the Rutherford Appleton Laboratory on the OPAL project in 1982. By 1987, he was Head of the particle physics department computing group and was subsequently appointed Head of the computing and resource management division in 1995. In 1999, while still at Rutherford Appleton Laboratory, he was also appointed Chairman of the CERN FOCUS committee, overseeing the CERN IT department.

Mr. Jeffreys was appointed an Oxford Fellow in 2001, a position he still holds. During this time, he has held memberships on several committees and programs, including e-Science Core Programme Grid Network Team and Technical Advisory Group, PPARC e-Science Oversight Panel, National Cancer Tissue Resource Project, and IBM World Community Grid Advisory Board.

Mr. Jeffreys is the author and coauthor of several publications on the topic of grid computing and biomolecular simulation.

About the Contributors

K. Vaman Kamath is the former Managing Director and CEO of ICICI Bank, Ltd., India's second-largest bank. Headquartered in Mumbai, ICICI is India's largest private bank with more than 1,250 branches and locations in more than 20 countries.

Mr. Kamath started his career in 1971 at ICICI, an Indian financial institution that founded the ICICI Bank and merged with it in 2002. In 1998, he moved to the Asian Development Bank and spent several years in Southeast Asia before returning to ICICI as CEO in 1996. Over the next years, the ICICI Group transformed itself into a diversified, technology-driven financial services group. Under Mr. Kamath's leadership, ICICI became the first Indian company and the second Asian bank to list on the New York Stock Exchange. Mr. Kamath retired from the company in 2009.

Mr. Kamath is a member of the governing board of various educational institutions and the *Economic Times* Editorial Advisory Board. In 2007, he was named Businessman of the Year by *Forbes Asia* and Business Leader of the Year by the *Economic Times*.

Ravi Kant is the Managing Director of Tata Motors, India's largest automobile company. In 2008, Tata unveiled the world's cheapest car.

Prior to joining Tata Motors, Mr. Kant served as Vice President, Sales and Marketing, at Titan Watches, the world's fifth largest and India's leading manufacturer of watches, and Senior Executive

Director, Marketing, at the Indian scooter company LML. He then served as Director, Consumer Electronics at Philips India, a leading brand in consumer and professional products.

Mr. Kant became a Director of Tata Motors in May 2000, with responsibilities for the manufacturing and marketing of commercial vehicles and the manufacturing of utility vehicles. He was appointed to Managing Director in July 2005 and now oversees the company's day-to-day operations.

Howard Lester is the Chairman and CEO of Williams-Sonoma, a premier specialty retailer of home furnishings and cooking supplies and equipment.

Mr. Lester has extensive experience in computer operations and spent fifteen years in the computer industry before entering retailing. After six years with Computer Sciences Corporation, he became Executive Vice President of Bradford National Corporation, which acquired Centurex.

Mr. Lester purchased Williams-Sonoma in 1978 and since then has held the positions of President, CEO, and Chairman.

Mr. Lester is also on the Executive Council of UCSF. He is on the advisory boards of the Retail Management Institute of Santa Clara University and the Walter A. Haas School of Business at the University of California, Berkeley.

He previously served on the boards of the Boy Scouts of America, Conner Peripherals Inc.,

About the Contributors

Harold's Stores Inc., and the International Association of Shopping Centers.

Jimmy Wales is the founder of Wikipedia, the free open-content encyclopedia.

From 1994 to 2000, Mr. Wales was the Research Director at Chicago Options Associates, a futures and options trading firm in Chicago. In 2000, he started the open-content encyclopedia Nupedia. In 2001, he founded Wikipedia, a free, online encyclopedia that anyone can edit.

Mr. Wales is the Chairman of Wikimedia Foundation Inc., a nonprofit charitable organization dedicated to encouraging the growth, development, and distribution of free, multilingual content. He is the cofounder of Wiki, Inc., a wiki farm that includes a collection of wikis on different topics, all hosted on the same site.

He is a Fellow at the Berkman Center for Internet and Society at Harvard Law School and a Director of Creative Commons, a nonprofit licensing organization.

In 2006, Mr. Wales was named as one of *Time* magazine's people who shape our world, and in 2007, he was named as a *Forbes* magazine Web celebrity.

Bruce Winzar is CIO of Australia's Loddon Mallee Rural Health Alliance and Executive Director of Information Services responsible for ICT, applications, and medical records at Bendigo Health Care Group.

About the Contributors

The Loddon Mallee Rural Health Alliance is one of five rural alliances operating under a joint venture agreement. Each publicly funded foundation member is involved in the provision of health services with the goal of improving their joint capability and capacity to use and acquire information and communications technology products and services and thereby improve provider and client services.

Bendigo Health Care Group is an expanding, multiservice, regional health organization and is the largest regional health provider in the state of Victoria. Bendigo Health traces its genesis to the establishment of a hospital in the goldfields in 1853, now operating hospitals, nursing homes, and health care centers. The group is the major referral hospital and health care provider in the Loddon-Mallee region, employing just under two thousand workers.

Mr. Winzar has been in the ICT industry since 1976 and has held several senior ICT roles in both the private and public sectors, including operating his own consulting service. He has held lead roles in specifying and supervising the delivery of new models for services in health and local government, and provided project management for a range of large projects.

Mr. Winzar was involved with the development of Australia's first regional telecommunications company in 1998 and was a board member for the first three years of its inception. He also managed the development of Central Victoria's Innovation

About the Contributors

Park and was inaugural chair of the Central Victorian ICT Cluster, a state government initiative to promote and develop the ICT industry in central Victoria.

With a passionate interest for the fair and equitable delivery of telecommunications services to the rural and remote sector of Australia, Mr. Winzar is a member of the Digital Economy Information Group for Health. His expertise covers business and management systems. He has worked across three tiers of government and facilitated a number of significant regional economic development initiatives for Central Victoria.

⌐ ACKNOWLEDGMENTS ⌐

First and foremost, a heartfelt thanks goes to all of the executives who have candidly shared their hard-won experience and battle-tested insights for the *Lessons Learned* series.

We thank IBM for permission to use lessons produced in partnership as part of two separate video series. The first was inspired by the IBM Global CEO Study, "The Enterprise of the Future." The second was inspired by the IBM Global CIO Study, "The New Voice of the CIO." For more information on IBM's market-leading C-Suite Studies, please visit www.ibm.com/gbs/cxo and www.ibm.com/voiceofthecio.

We thank the Center for CIO Leadership for permission to use lessons produced in partnership for its Web site, www.cioleadershipcenter.com.

Angelia Herrin at Harvard Business Publishing consistently offered unwavering support, good humor, and counsel from the inception of this ambitious project.

Kathleen Carr, Brian Surette, and David Goehring provided invaluable editorial direction, perspective, and encouragement, particularly for this second series. Many thanks to the entire HBP team of designers, copy editors, and marketing professionals who helped bring this series to life.

Acknowledgments

Much appreciation goes to Jennifer Lynn and Christopher Benoît for research and diligent attention to detail, and to Roberto de Vicq de Cumptich for his imaginative cover designs.

Finally, thanks to James MacKinnon and the entire 50 Lessons team for their time, effort, and steadfast support of this project.

THE LAST PAGE IS
ONLY THE BEGINNING

Watch Free *Lessons Learned*
Video Interviews and Get Additional Resources

You've just read first-hand accounts from the business
world's top leaders, but the learning doesn't have to
end there. 50 Lessons gives you access to:

**Exclusive videos featuring the leaders
profiled in this book**

**Practical advice for putting their
insights into action**

**Challenging questions that
extend your learning**

FREE ONLINE AT:
www.50lessons.com/technology